Shame | Shame

❖ ❖ ❖

Winner, 2014 A. Poulin, Jr. Poetry Prize

Selected by David St. John

Shame | Shame

❖ ❖ ❖

POEMS BY

DEVIN BECKER

FOREWORD BY DAVID ST. JOHN

A. POULIN, JR. NEW POETS OF AMERICA SERIES, NO. 37

BOA Editions, Ltd. ❖ Rochester, NY ❖ 2015

First Edition
15 16 17 18   7 6 5 4 3 2 1

For information about permission to reuse any material from this book please contact The
Permissions Company at www.permissionscompany.com or e-mail permdude@eclipse.net.

Publications by BOA Editions, Ltd.—a not-for-profit corporation
under section 501 (c) (3) of the United States Internal Revenue
Code—are made possible with funds from a variety of sources,
including public funds from the New York State Council on the
Arts, a state agency; the Literature Program of the National En-
dowment for the Arts; the County of Monroe, NY; the Lannan
Foundation for support of the Lannan Translations Selection Se-
ries; the Mary S. Mulligan Charitable Trust; the Rochester Area
Community Foundation; the Arts & Cultural Council for Greater
Rochester; the Steeple-Jack Fund; the Ames-Amzalak Memorial
Trust in memory of Henry Ames, Semon Amzalak and Dan Amzalak; and contributions
from many individuals nationwide. See Colophon on page 72 for special individual
acknowledgments.

ART WORKS.
arts.gov

State of the Arts

NYSCA

Cover Design: Sandy Knight
Interior Design and Composition: Richard Foerster
Manufacturing: Versa Press, Inc.
BOA Logo: Mirko

Library of Congress Cataloging-in-Publication Data

Becker, Devin.
 [Poems. Selections]
 Shame | Shame : poems / by Devin Becker ; Foreword by David St. John — First
Edition.
     pages cm. — (A. Poulin, Jr. New Poets of America Series, no. 37)
 ISBN 978-1-938160-59-2 (pbk. : alk. paper) — ISBN 978-1-938160-60-8 (ebook)
PS3602.E2894A6 2015
811'.6—dc23
                          2014040080

BOA Editions, Ltd.
250 North Goodman Street, Suite 306
Rochester, NY 14607
www.boaeditions.org
A. Poulin, Jr., Founder (1938–1996)

Contents

❖ ❖ ❖

Foreword

Devin Becker's *Shame | Shame* is a brilliant debut collection. Here, the prose poem has been reimagined as a cinematic vignette, yet rooted as deeply in the American Northwest as anything in Richard Hugo and David Lynch. Raw, intimate, and elliptical in its metaphysics, Devin Becker's poetry captures an idiomatic recklessness while navigating those angular narratives of our contemporary lives. As Becker says at the conclusion of one of his many exquisitely self-eviscerating poems: "Reader, this is Trouble. / He's new here. / Don't be nice to him."

This collection interrogates mythic American convictions and ideals, those virtues and lies upon which we've built a culture. Throughout its history, our country has reflected upon those who've escaped West to reinvent themselves, to escape their pasts, and to hide from that sense of an imposed social or class fate. For once, a book seems well served by its main epigraph. Becker has chosen a passage from Simone Weil that underscores the conflicting forces at work upon any individual. As you read this passage after reading Devin Becker's poems, you understand it as a startling précis of what the speaker of these poems faces in even the most ordinary aspects of his daily life. We all want to know what happened to Huck after he decided to "light out for the Territory"—my own sense is that 150 years later, a little sadder and a whole lot wiser, he emerged as Devin Becker.

Although his prose poem vignettes dominate much of *Shame | Shame*—look to the poem "Mirror-Stage" for notes on this choice—Devin Becker is equally adept at carving precisely lineated poems, and each stylistic inclination has its virtues. The prose poem vignettes are each a kind of startling elliptical playlet, a cinematic reflection in verse (yes, this prose is verse) in which the metaphorical turns metaphysical more often than not. Becker is remarkable in his ability to sketch the delicate shifts of unstable human weathers. Over and over in these poems, our human failings become not failings, merely human.

Likewise, the physical landscapes in these poems seem to embrace the loneliness of these figures even as they are stripped naked in their fears. Becker excels at revealing to us what is often remarkably intimate within what we understand to be a public—social or professional—situation or occasion. There is an odd yet deeply tender familiarity to this work, as in those scenes from the early films of Truffaut or Goddard. The cinematic composure in Devin Becker's poetry drew me within it time and time again, making me feel, as a reader, as vulnerable as his speakers.

There are also moments of ethical free-fall in these poems, moments that begin as wry moral reflections and resolve as both personal and cultural self-indictments. The range of poetic vision that surveys these discrete and precisely described locales is, in fact, panoramic. Becker has the rapturous eye of a cinematographer and the incisive—even eviscerating—instincts of a superb playwright. The mirrors of embarrassment surround us at every moment in *Shame | Shame*, and Becker wants us to see ourselves within them in order to consider, as his speaker does, how we might make choices that could yet reflect whatever values we might still aspire to in our lives. Disabused of our self-righteous fantasies about ourselves, we have at the very least these fables of forgiveness—both of ourselves and those around us—that populate this stunning collection. Just as sunlight through a magnifying glass sets tinder afire, so too the lens of Devin Becker's poetry, allowing every shame to burst suddenly into brilliant and illuminating flames.

—David St. John

❖ ❖ ❖

. . . the question of what elements in the soul are transformed by merciless necessity as it tailors the soul to fit the requirements of shifting fate, and of what elements can on the other hand be preserved through the exercise of virtue and through grace—this whole question is fraught with temptations to falsehood, temptations that are positively enhanced by pride, by shame, by hatred, contempt, indifference, by the will to oblivion or to ignorance.

—Simone Weil, "The *Iliad,* or the Poem of Force"

Fate is the present desperado.

—Wallace Stevens

Western

In one sense, "No One" is also a type of dream job, and all my life I've heard him calling from the inside: *What is love*, he asks, *save something one is in, like trouble.*

No One is also a type of American everyone loves—

He wakes up in the morning alive, having won the fight, fucked.

But the demands of character are such he must leave, or else risk saying Yes to possibilities he will lose what he loves.

Too recently I remember thinking, if I only dressed more like Dave, I could blend in totally, no one would notice me, and *How much more of an impression I could make from there when I emerged.*

So I let my friends turn to acquaintances; I refined the solitude sequences; and I waited, but my hero's entrance never cued up.

I ask: for this, have I abandoned my loves?

No One says, *Son, if you blow your brains out they will come—*

I ask: Whose is this salesman's voice in me that wants me gone?

Smoothie Joint

Idaho. Everyone is nice. Which of course makes me super uneasy. And the men all have these huge, meat-red hands. Ribeye-colored, every one of them.

Kristin and I have been driving all day, exploring the smaller towns around our new one. And the trip's been good—we befriended Mel, a used bookstore owner; I saw a snake and it didn't bite me—but we're tired now, so we decide we'll get some ice cream in the next town, then head home.

Ice cream turns out to be a really delicious "all juice" smoothie and a cookie, which we eat outside in the sun with a local paper, scanning the ads.

It is almost four by now, almost time for the little smoothie joint to close, and so as not to be a bother to the workers, I decide we should take our plates in, and the paper.

Kristin goes in first and hands our plates to the man who made our smoothie and when I go in a minute later to throw the newspaper away, he is still near the entrance, cleaning a table.

He looks at me.

I ask, "It's okay to throw away the paper, right?"

He doesn't say anything for a while.

Then he says, all serious, "Today's paper?" pausing for several moments after.

Then he laughs. Not haughtily but close. Almost haughtily.

Nervously I tell him how good the smoothie was. (It *was* exceptional.)

He says, "All Juice."

"Crazy," I say.

"Yeah. Thanks," he says.

Tennis Courts

The boys, both in their early teens, are brothers. You can tell by their limbs. Their father sits on the bench outside the tennis courts watching them hit serves, saying, "Bend your knees." "Extend."

As they finish the last bucket a man on a bicycle stops next to their father and begins telling him about his own history as a tennis player, detailing the tenuous connections he has to the better players in the area, even a few of the professionals.

The man is obviously high, or fried from being high all the time. He talks too loudly. But the boys' father listens to him politely, engaging him when he recognizes a name, and the boys, after they finish picking up the tennis balls, sit down on either side of their father and listen too, indistinguishable from each other.

The man on his bicycle is surprised by this, to have them listening. In turn, he excuses himself, claiming he has to be somewhere, at work.

The boys and their father load up their car and leave.

The man comes back after they're gone and rides his bicycle around the tennis courts giggling, bespectacled, and shirtless.

Tobacco Outlet

I resist myself almost successfully for about an hour, have a strong beer to reward my discipline, then, the alcohol helping (if that is the word), stop resisting the urge to, hop in the car, and drive a mile or so up to where the interstate exits are to buy some cigarettes.

I am not disappointed in myself for doing this.

The ride over itself is worth it: the wind is warm, sustained; it pushes the trees' limbs into weird symmetries, flips their leaves up so they flash pale against the evening.

Earlier a storm came through so fallen branches litter the fields and in the parking lot of the tobacco outlet, a downed wire hangs low across a row of poorly outlined spaces.

With the windshield of my car, I hit the wire, gently, accidentally, not seeing it even though someone has tied a few white paper bags around the wire as a warning (a job I would have declined).

I back my car up and park in another spot.

I'm embarrassed when I enter the store, and a little lightheaded from the beer.

Marlboro Lights, I say.

Box? asks the cashier.

A bored man behind her warns me about the wire. I can't tell if he's already seen me hit it. I thank him. I drive off with my windows down and the soft wind.

Back home, I get out a folding chair, set it down in the middle of the lawn, and smoke.

The chair is sturdy. The cigarette smells like my grandmother.

Three skunks—a mother and two babies—waddle onto a patch of grass bordering the woods. I do not want to be, but I'm afraid of them, so I put out my cigarette in the grass and go back in.

Backyard

My neighbor's little dog, Noodle, comes running toward me inquisitive and then angry, barking, surprised to discover I'm a person.

(Maybe her vision is no good.)

I get up and say, Hey Noodle.

Then my neighbor, a mid-twenties grad-student guy in a yellow shirt, blue shorts, and black socks, comes and gets his dog.

Noodle *come*, he says.

I'm on the phone the whole time so I can't really talk to him, although I want to ask him how he's doing, how he and his girlfriend are settling in.

We've only known each other a week, and have only spoken once really. And I think we will all like each other, but he and his girlfriend and me and mine have somehow already created a great deal of awkwardness between us, just by respecting one another's privacy.

My friend Jeff is on the phone. His girlfriend, Kelly, just broke up with him; she cut her trip to Houston short, leaving five days before the agreed-upon seventeen were over.

I want to comfort Jeff but I can't, can't tell him anything really because each thing I tell him only makes him realize more how much he needs Kelly to say something other than that which his pleading is forcing her to keep on saying. (It's over.)

And Jeff's broken heart is not beautiful; it's awkward, off-putting, hard for either of us to acknowledge, and yet the automaton Jeff becomes, playing "the Unrequited," is comforting, too, as his predictability implies there's a similarity at base among all of us.

Regardless, Jeff is Jeff and Kelly is Kelly and Noodle is Noodle. And these are irrefutable, irreconcilable.

I cannot convince Jeff of any of this though, although he wants me to.

Restaurant

"You must change your life" pops up again. As it always does. A slogan from his twenties repeated, pondered upon, rejected, accepted, never really followed.

Also he thinks of the little square books they sold at Barnes & Noble, on the counter, Rilke again, *Letters to a Young Poet*. How disappointed he was when he read one again a few years ago, that book which had promised him nothing, he realized, which had warned him, if anything, against this life.

I'm learned I'm learned, he mocks himself.

Fuck. I'm fucked.

Fuck You.

No, no.

He takes a sip from the glossy water glass and looks off at the little candles flickering on the wine shelves. Here, his hands on the bar, waiting for his cheese and honey plate, a beer and this water glass in front of him. Here, in the moment he's overly conscious of.

Your thoughts are embarrassing.

"If it is to be believable, to be effective in evoking some emotion in a reader, the conclusion must be simple, inevitable."

This is what he teaches!

"And if it is to succeed as such, a story must include Trouble, that character whose rift the author must, like a musician, resolve."

Reader, this is Trouble.
He's new here.
Don't be nice to him.

Data

If you believe everything is data, a pulsing sphere of inputs and outputs feeding off each other—circumstance being both the mold and what is molded—an act of Terrorism (that constant), however gratuitous, must be considered a kind of natural disaster, as it is, at base, a release, from the system, of a tension built by the rubbing together of opposite and incongruous desires.

One birthday, ever the Protestant, I decided I should remind myself the world suffered while I celebrated, so I downloaded the lead *New York Times* photo—an Iraqi woman crying over the charred spot where her boy had perished—and let it devastate me for a while.

Now it's stored with my other image files—paintings I like, photos from bars, etc.—and like them, it comes up sometimes on my screensaver.

I'm so used to it now, I barely see it anymore—the charred spot like a brushstroke, her white teeth above the black O of her open mouth. The scene floats by without charge; the shock of it used up when? That first day?

(My life consumed by itself, myself, my data. My dataset, my healthy dataset—)

When the photo comes up with guests over and someone notices, I use the occasion to anecdote about my Midwestern/Protestant guilt-ethic.

Oh and we laugh. We laugh for what seems ages.

Auditorium

Into this horrible auditorium, its chairs proportioned into two, too-wide phalanxes. And what is not gray in here is a yellow-brown. And what is not covered by chairs is a rubbery surface—the kind that floors gymnasiums the school-world over.

I sit in back, two rows behind my coworkers, one of whom notices then chides me for sitting back here "like a teenager."

I *am* a teenager, is what I want to say.

Instead I say I didn't realize. Sorry.

And truly I just want to feel I can escape if I have to, my panic having become, lately, almost constant, likely to emerge at any formal moment, even the most mundane.

I dressed for this, this meeting, the "Introduction of New Faculty." I picked out a shirt I thought would seem a bit more fashionable than the others'; wore my nice khakis.

The different disciplines are clumped around and in front of me: the anthropologists looking a bit unfurled; the engineers, generic—

I don't really feel I belong here, but I don't feel anyone else does either, save for the business professors, both of whom are unbelievably, unsettlingly tan.

The administrators are first. My new boss stands and does this stupid wave where he keeps his elbow tucked against his sides and shrugs his shoulders. Then the Art Department hires are introduced, the Business folk, the Agriculture profs, etc. Finally, after the ROTC Colonels, they get to the Librarians.

I stand and do the same wave my boss did, shrugging, my elbow in and my eyes trained on the floor, my too-big shirt billowing up when I sit, ballooning.

Me, the balloon.

Breakfast Bar

Truth has been replaced by Narrative, is what the eggheads say. I say: the peregrinations time holds for us are relentlessly forward.

(Should I go to LA? I should go to LA.)

And furthermore, to oppose these systems is not the point; the point is to be aware that everyone and every system is out to get you.

(Sometimes I find too many vegetables ruin the omelet; sometimes, the opposite.)

To theorize is to direct traffic with your elbow.

(To atomize is to need a magnifier.)

The problem with endings is that they end and still you have to find someone who will love you for you and despite the future.

(A future whose promise is so powerful we live by repressing the dread it inspires.)

The problem with criticism of any kind is that it assumes artists capable of and therefore either progressing toward or declining from their "full potential."

(I am full of eggs and broccoli this morning. Later I will be less full.)

This is true also of psychiatrists. You must separate your self from your anxiety, the Shrink says; Critic: you are too in love with your own style.

Business School

Linnea, Geoff, and I go to the smaller coffee shop in the Admin Building. We get lattes. And it's still warm enough to sit outside, so we do, on the edges of these triangular concrete plantings installed haphazardly near the Business School.

Halloween is coming so Geoff describes his costume to us—a villain from some video game, thick scar down the left side of his face, through his eye.

I ask if both of them are going to Ben's party.

Linnea says, "Ben's having a party?" which is awful, which is a little taste of bile.

Geoff, in his goodness, tells Linnea she can be his +1 if she wants to.

Linnea says she's kind of a recluse anyway. (I shouldn't feel bad.) She likes to watch movies, have a glass of wine by herself, in her own house.

I miss the party too. The next Monday I hear Geoff's costume was spectacular, that the all-white contact he wore in his left eye—the one he complained that day was so painful to insert—looked real, frightened Ben's kid.

Living Room

I am kind of hoping these two women will sleep with me, but really I'd rather be alone and done with the tawdry part of my life. And that the possibility is even there has me sort of frozen. Partly I realize just getting to this point is probably better than going through with anything, the logistics.

One of the women and I slept together about a year ago. A bunch of us stayed at a friend's house after a wedding and she plopped down next to me after I set up a little bed of covers for myself on the faux-shag carpet. Tawdry for sure, but good too, necessary—and lovely in the way oblivion is a type of love, or a part, at least, comfort to the new and ex- lover both in that it's visceral, proof of something, some thing.

(*Ex nihilo,* maybe.)

Maybe that's where shame comes from: something visceral from the *nothing there* emerges and you want to cover it—the fig leaf I wanted that morning when she sat on my lap in front of our friends.

New Year's Eve Day

I'm in the workout facility of the subdivision Kristin's parents live in and it's me, this older couple, and a redheaded high school girl wearing a pink T-shirt with "Red" handwritten on the back of it.

None of us can work the televisions so we're surrounded by black rectangles, but I've got an audio book so I'm semi-entertained. On the elliptical, I move my feet up and down smoothly in short strides listening to Johnny Depp read Keith Richard's autobiography, my general hope being that I'll sweat and lose weight and look better and have a more clearly-defined jaw line.

I can tell Red wants to use the elliptical but I don't want to get off it yet, so she uses this ab-stand thing halfheartedly while the older man and woman walk the two treadmills at their slowest speeds.

I get done, Red takes my place, then I take hers on the ab-stand.

I lift my legs up to my chest nineteen times.

The older woman comes over as I'm finishing and remarks that today's the first time she's ever seen someone use that thing and oh to be young like me and Red.

Red is way younger than me I think and then I think about dying, I get that twinge.

The older couple leaves and it's just me and Red and a sort of tension emerges but it's not sexual; it's annoyance.

I finish up and change to walk back to Kristin's parents' house. I wish Red a happy New Year on the way out after debating in the locker room whether doing so would be creepy or appropriate.

I walk back along the road, houses on one side, late December mudfields for miles on the other.

Some guy working on a car in his garage looks at me weird, so noncommittally I say, "Howdy."

Corner Club

Some large men hate small men, especially at bars. We remind them the world is not just full of men like them, that it also contains smaller, more delicate varieties—

Ryan's with me. We're both small, but he's trying to keep up with these two probably 300-pounders while I'm just trying to ignore everything and watch football, although the shots and the fifty ounces of Bud Light I've sipped in the past two hours have reduced my attention span to this sort of constant flit where I'm relying less on live events and more on replays.

This 85-year-old guy Francis sits on my other side. He definitely hates me, but he hates everyone, so it's no big deal.

A shot appears in front of me. Ryan's ordered it.

I ask what's in the shot, so the one big guy snorts: *A man doesn't ask what's in a shot, he takes it*, pausing after for my retort, smiling his giant teeth.

That's what my mom says, I offer; receive awkward looks.

I take the shot. No one gives a shit.

I am really starting to love football, the punishment of it.

Butte

Why, Memory, why focus on the shirt, on its white, how it was not white, but gray, grayish?

It speaks to your lack of character. You are a careless launderer.

But I thought maybe once about the shirt that whole day.

I am nothing if not instructive.

There was no path. We just parked the car and walked right up the butte. I called it "the butt" and she laughed.

She was embarrassed for you. You have no idea how painful it is to watch you pepper your interactions with "humor."

Seriously? What should I do then? Reminisce? Any time I pause you unspool me toward some embarrassment.

Discomfort is requisite, if instruction is to hold. And you produce enough reverie for twenty men, you need more?

But my shirt, really? I can barely remember the top, or how scared we were at coming upon the herd of elk hidden in the trees.

They just stood there, like cows. Maybe they were cows.

They were not cows.

Sangria

These two couples are sharing a pitcher of sangria and the girls are pleasuring each other, going back and forth, each in turn claiming herself fatter.

I'm the cow, one says.

No, I AM, replies the other.

They are all so young they're just practicing for later, but OMyFuckingGod they want it now, Lord, they are DYING to get comfortable.

Were it that each could, but the one boy's eyes are uneven and his girlfriend is actually a fair bit bigger than the other's, so the feelings between the couples dim a little after the banter stops and their physical inequities start to glare across the table.

The restaurant is jungle-themed, bamboo everywhere with little leaves hanging down, and in the quiet just created, the better-looking boy starts to pull a branch apart until he notices their waitress returning.

Time for dessert now, Fatty, he says to his girlfriend, the skinny one.

And the kindness with which he says this forgives everyone, all of us; cleans the room.

Atlantic City

Garish as it is, the room's pride is its own and it only cost thirty-nine dollars, total, so we are, each of us, happy to be in it, in Atlantic City, on a Monday in the middle of March, looking out from our window at the ocean, drinking 40s we bought on our way in from a liquor store in the more frightening part of town.

Problem is there's only one bed, three of us, and then this weird little bench thing beneath a window, so we decide whoever loses rock-paper-scissors will have to sleep on the bench thing.

Jacob loses, but Gabe gets so drunk he just sleeps on it anyway.

We wake up in the morning and find the place with the cheese-steaks, the White House, then all three of us get into Gabe's shitty little Toyota and start driving back to Baltimore.

We stink, each of us, and we know it, although Jacob's stink is somehow greater than mine or Gabe's, earthier, at once more impressive and more off-putting, disgusting in the way sometimes heights are disgusting—that brief, pelvic shock of oneself, precarious in comparison.

So Gabe tells Jacob he smells like a communist.

Whoa, Jacob says. *Whoa.*

The Internet

Everything is okay.
The divorce plays out on Facebook.   (High Resolution)
His last tweet goes viral.   (Fame, finally)
I search-box an old flame
to commune with her About Page.   (Her true body)
Everything far is close.   (Everything close, far)
But every hour for ten minutes
you must stop what you're doing   (your eyes about to ruin)
and look into the distance.   (Lest pixelation square you)
Do this often.

                    (Often in remembrance)

Apartment

I get so drunk, on bourbon, so many nights in a row, alone, applying for graduate school, I develop a bad cold despite not, to my knowledge, coming into contact with anyone for at least a week, prior.

And I find my getting sick unbelievable, scientifically, but the cold is undeniable, as is my drinking problem, which is not so pronounced or embarrassing as it could be, granted, but exists and tires me nonetheless.

It had my uncle worse than it has me. Had him through and to the accident he ended in, that ended him.

Cleaning out his apartment after with some family, I found his living room familiar. The ashtrays and bottles seemed haphazard to the others, but I saw structure, a concision—table, chair, TV, all in a row—meant, like all minimalism, to smooth the viewer down and out, efficiently.

Increasingly unsophisticated receptor.

TV, booze, recliner, smokes: Operation Freedom.

Space Shuttle Endeavor.

Conference

This guy Mark obviously knows more about Information Technology than I do, but we're at the same conference and I'm networking so I introduce myself, telling him, fake-confidentially, I have no clue what anyone is saying.

Mark is annoyed, but polite. We both realize there are more important people he should be talking to, but he does me the courtesy of discussing something from the last session and then excuses himself in order to read the listings for the next.

I am not a total idiot so I walk a good fifteen feet over to the coffee and Mark goes a little bit in the opposite direction, looks intently at his program.

The carpet has one of those diagonal plaid designs on it and I follow one of the lines for a while, thinking how much this feels like college.

I remember smoking a cigarette one weekend night outside my dorm and these more popular guys walking by, one of them saying something nasty to me.

Little bitch, he called me.

(No reason, really. Or maybe a hundred, I don't know.)

And then the other guy: *He's drunk, dude. Sorry.*

Apology almost as stunning as the insult.

I went back inside to my little room after, shut down my computer, got in bed. Not sad. Confused, angry.

Indianapolis

Strip mall bars are DUI factories. I'm not driving, thank God; someone else has to worry.

(Or maybe they don't worry. Maybe *that's* the difference.)

It feels good, regardless, being out of Fort Wayne for a night, even if we're spending it at this shitty bar and it's hot as balls outside on this sidewalk patio where we're smoking and where I'm wearing a long-sleeve shirt to cover up some poison ivy.

Michael drove us down here this morning so we could get drunk with his college friends, guys I know a little, some of whom I grew up with.

On the patio, he asks to see my arms. I show him. Gross, he says.

We have a few more beers at the bar then drive back to someone's house and play drinking games until we pass out. The next day I wake up in the late morning on the dining room floor still in my shirt. I go sit at the kitchen table.

Outside the wind is rippling the man-made pond this block of homes is built around. There are some geese, but geese are everywhere.

Geese have no morals.

Kristin

I let Kristin read one, not one she's mentioned in, or the sex one, the one where I get drunk, with Michael, at a strip mall.

She doesn't like it.

She says *Geese have no morals* sounds like an ending and she doesn't like that sound, the wrap-up.

I tell her there is much written on the subject (see Hejinian), and I know what she's saying, but I like the geese part, it sounds like an ending but it's not: obviously the guy (me!) is still conflicted, unresolved.

And I thought these would be more mundane, more about *anyone*, she tells me, at least from what you've said.

I tell her I can't resist myself, I'm sorry, all the while seething, thinking *why the fuck can't you give me even the slightest praise.*

Ridiculous, how much I've built my life toward this, toward praise, how much I go searching for it, need it, need more of it.

And in my head I blame everyone for this, even America, but Kristin doesn't see this about me, which is maybe why she can talk to me like she does: not coldly, honestly, astonishingly.

Wedding

Daniel, our DJ, is having personal problems. He tells me when I pick him up the-morning-of that his wife left him for good on Thursday, taking the car.

He says he was a wreck the morning of his wedding, and that on Thursday he and his now gone-for-good wife went swimming, split a bottle of champagne, then said goodbye to each other.

And so on this, my morning-of, I am at Daniel's new, clean, and depressingly small apartment in order to drive him and his DJ setup to the reception venue, his soon-to-be ex-wife having taken the car.

And these personal problems Daniel is having, he's been having all summer: In June, his "recommended" shelf at the video store (his day job) morphed from a scattering of hip-hop documentaries into a solid row of breakup movies.

We thought little of this at the time other than "poor Daniel," which is what I am thinking again now, at 10:30 AM, listening to him tell me about his wife and swimming with her at the reservoir, just hours before she left him, and town.

I am also thinking that later, probably during the ceremony, I will lose control of my bladder and soil myself.

Daniel offers me a scotch—he drank scotch on *his* morning-of apparently—but too anxious to give up control of anything, I don't take him up on it, though later, at the reception, I will drink my share and Daniel will have his starting time pushed back an hour by the dinner service, which is another thing about which Daniel will be unhappy, and all this misfortune will then express itself in his song selection: a series of off-putting '90s dance tunes that will be kind of what I feared and kind of what I hoped for.

I'll tell our guests the next day at brunch that Daniel, our DJ, was having personal problems: On Thursday, his wife left him.

My mom will still be angry months later, and Kristin and I will avoid the video store for a while after, but it's a small town and we will still like Daniel. His summer (our summer-of) was not one we would wish for, or on, anyone.

And not one we would think about except it's hard not to.

Nook

None of us wins the conversations we imagine having with assholes.

We are so bad at them.

We say the wrong words at the wrong times in the wrong cadences.

And the assholes are like, "Really?"

And we're like "maybe if you weren't such ASSHOLES . . ."

But that's exactly what Assholes want: for us to call them by name in all caps then dot-dot-dot, aka ellipsis.

I can't decide if my hating them is sin or virtue, if I should hate them specifically or hate their asshole-ness.

I'm not alone in this; big religions come down on both sides of both questions. But I don't trust big religions, I prefer little ones, like Reading.

Reading says, *None of us, not one of us, is alone.*

Reading says, *We are speaking to each other even now from our little homes.*

I am in my nook, my head framed by the fake window cut out from the drywall. Kristin is at the kitchen table working on her computer. You are welcome to be here for a while, but you should leave at some point, for our own goods.

Oh my god, the assholes are so bored right now.

They are like what the fuck is that pussy talking about.

Plot

I was missing a funeral, literally, and so
Death is what I was thinking about,
figuratively: the swift hammer stroke of it,
if you're lucky,
& the shitty-home-repairman's-thousand-little-misaimed-whacks,
if you're not.

And I was getting a little correlative buzz
from this, from
focusing on the differences between
me and dead men.
I stared at the bar of light slipping out under the bathroom door and felt
ecstatically, shamefully lucky.

It was early, too early,
so after peeing and drinking some water I went back to bed and
when I got in, Kristin asked me "How are you?" and I said
"I am alive," softly
but with conviction, I thought,
although then Kristin asked, "That's all?"
so I had to tell her
"That's pretty good."

The sun was coming up 2000 miles east of us
where the funeral was and I thought it might be
leaking into our sky a little because
outside I saw purple, which is the color of grace,
I remembered from when I was a kid in church and
we'd have to make purple banners each Easter to hang on the
A-frame walls of the sanctuary.

And the dead man being tall,
he helped us hang them.

Water Fountain

After someone

I don't remember what we fought about near the water fountain.

I don't remember the way the air felt on my skin in the winter when my sled slid out off the bank and skidded across the river.

I don't remember the taste of watermelon in the summer. Watermelon in any season.

I don't remember the conversation we had about recreational vehicles nor our discussing the wonderful future that awaited us in them, but she does.

I don't remember how it felt to have my beard peeled off after playing Moses in the school play when I was seven. I remember my director telling me it would sting.

I don't remember my first time really panicking for no reason.

I don't remember what the ladies my mom played bridge with liked to talk about when I eavesdropped on them but I remember wanting to try their daiquiris.

I don't remember what we were looking for in the files I flipped through endlessly that whole fall, listening to public radio.

I don't remember blacking out after the baseball hit me in the forehead but the palpable relief I remember seeing on the face of my father upon coming-to is lovely to me still.

I don't remember how I felt on first seeing Kristin. On first hearing her voice, on the cell phone, I felt annoyed.

I don't remember really liking Jim's reading of the Q&A section of

Ulysses, although his reading of the Moocow opening of *Portrait* is one of the top three literary moments of my life.

I don't remember the other two.

I don't remember Kristin's phone number. (It's in my phone.) My mother's voice inside me tells me I should memorize it for emergencies.

I don't remember the code in Mortal Kombat that would make the one character pull the spine out of his opponent after a victory.

I don't remember anything useful.

Like how purely Me I felt when I was young and it was my birthday. I remember the view coming down from the stairs in the morning.

I don't remember caring much about money before, although now it feels like this game where I'm losing.

Parking Lot

I am looking for a spot that will retain no meaning, no charge. So I drive her to a dentist's office—not my dentist, not hers—and in the parking lot I tell her it's over, the whole thing. I tell her our relationship "is untenable."

We look out the windshield into the office, the rooms all fluorescent, those horrible, reclined chairs, and white, white everywhere.

She tells me this just proves what she's always thought, what she believes on "a very personal level," that she's "a character actor in her own life."

It's a phrase she's been savoring, I realize, and so accurate a description I'm surprised she hasn't told me sooner, during a lull in one of our many restaurant dinners.

But I would have lied and told her it wasn't true, and she didn't want to be unconvinced of it, her revelation.

> (And what, asks the protagonist, is so
> bad about being a character actor?
> *Everyone steals from you.*)

Some security guy drives past us so I start the car up, relieved to have a reason.

He's got these scraggly whiskers that hang inches off his cheeks, and as he passes, he gives me a look.

This is his spot, I think. We're in his spot.

Window

Murder-Suicide describes, clearly, an act that, historically, has been considered more romantic than abhorrent.

And doubly 'romantic' besides in that it expresses, semantically speaking, both the sentimental and idealistic senses of the word.

All this, and yet Murder-Suicide connects, calmly, two very anti-human acts, and the clarity of the term, astounding in how little wiggle it seems to offer, gives way when one considers criteria such as motive, or duration.

For instance, how much time between murder and suicide is allowed before the two acts can no longer be hyphenated, merged?

A day? A month?

And what sort of causal relationship must be established?

Take our own, recent example:

Two weeks ago today, Ernesto Bustamante, a recently fired professor of psychology, shot his former student and lover, Katy Benoit, a total of thirteen times on her front porch and then fled to a hotel where, nine hours later and only upon being confronted by the police, he picked up one of his many guns, stuck it below his chin, and pulled the trigger.

Was this, as it is reported, a murder-suicide proper?

If Bustamante had escaped from town, had not been confronted by police for days afterwards, and only then, during a similar siege, had he ended himself the same way, would we connect these acts so firmly? Would we hyphenate them?

Regardless, immediately and now, now, and thus forever, the act by which Benoit's life was ended and that other that ended her murderer's will be indelibly connected.

Such a feeding on the story in those early days, the Internet pulsing with Professor Student Sexual Psychopathic Beast Killer.

"Bustamante Benoit murder-suicide"

And the house Benoit died outside of was circumscribed in yellow tape for awhile but now the tape is down and the house is still a house: they're not razing it.

Meanwhile the suicide room has been blacked over, literally, a black plastic sheet covering up the window through which cops sent tear gas before entering.

Fifth room down from the end nearest the convention center, second floor.

Room 213, says the affidavit.

The affidavit says the police found in Bustamante's room the following prescriptions: Clonazepam, Lexapro, Lamotrigine, Alprazolam.

As well a total of 6 handguns and revolvers, and, in his trunk, according to rumor, an unreported but large number of rifles and shotguns, causing people here to wonder if the plan were Murder-Murder-Murder-Murder-Murder-Murder-Suicide.

And still it persists, the Shakespearean sense of it: murder-suicide as a torrid pact between lovers, a bang-bang proposition forced by fate upon a pair so perfect the world could not abide them.

Persists even though implying a 1 to 1 equation in the agreement between murder-suicide participants is, I would guess, rarely if ever accurate.

Or maybe accurate in the way 13 bullets are accurate.

Northern Hemisphere

Maybe Orion's peeing on us, every night, horizon to horizon.

Just one big invisible star-dust piss stream splashing over all of us and his giant quasar-pocked face laughing, or not even laughing because what does he care.

What Leave I Offer

Lord,
which lets me walk by the river . . .
—Peter Cole

Consider it an amusement of the failure:
was out late walking when the blowhard:
the *portential* with which both she and the news
arrived in consequential order.

What is all this in the meantime and talking about?
Get to the me-time.

Escalator on which I,
office park where we,

the holiness of our mornings after:
your hair
frizzed out like a doll pony's.

We had such *mundaneity*;
were so *quitodian*.

Was it better to appear
to be intentioned, clear
as the author photo he depicted,
clean as the dickens?

Sad, Outside, Winter

I am sad
I am old,

each moment
now more

palimpsest
than imprint,

less
pin-pricked

exuberance
at being

underdressed
outside

than memory
of.

Did We Learn Anxiety from Each Other?

Or were we merely prone to it?

Do we form a choir? A chorus?

An exquisite corpse of loneliness? (Loneliness being the corpse's only subject . . .)

Is there a progenitor, for instance such as the world's first vampire, and if we could go back in time would we kill that person?

Or is it worth it? Are these abstractions of our bodies' Flight Responses good for us, some course of lessons?

Will the panic Panic teaches us someday rescue us from drowning as the river churns us and the boat seals us under?

Or will we embrace and go down together, estranged lovers in hospice meeting again, abandoning our deathbeds for the lobby couches?

Sleeping Next to a Lion

for Nicole, with whom I have difficulty getting a word in

It was late; she had to pee.
Woke up around 2, my bladder bursting, she said.
On Safari in Uganda,

the toilet she woke to find was
I swear, a folding chair with the seat cut out.
There were I guess you call them servants, no,

they WERE servants. Servants.
The servants said Lions think tents' sides walls
so when I heard a growl outside I knew

I couldn't move,
couldn't make any noise, cough, nothing—
or I would wake the lion

to the flesh nearby him and *be the cause*
both of my own death
and the death of the fifteen-year-old girl

sharing the tent with me.
Neither could she pee herself for fear the lion—
just six inches from my face, remember—

for fear the lion would ascertain
olfactorily—*by smell—*
the weakness of the barrier between them.

Six hours my bladder, bursting, and
don't get me wrong it was horrible
but it was also something, you know.

And the relief of that next morning, God—

The New Poetry

Where shall wisdom be found? Bloom asks.

(Not Leopold)

In numbers, Harold. Numbers.

Interactive bar graphs are the new poetry.

My anecdotes about smoothies are symptomatic, if anything, of a pox upon the whole scene, the whole genre.

Why so down this morning?

How to put this quantitatively: too many bad inputs; not enough good ones.

Let the x dimension be time and y mark my mood quality, good being on top. I am a line of loops going downward, medium to bad, each complaint a gasp to pump me up a bit, but then pulling me down even further.

Poems, watch out. Here come Charts.

Bloom: *Here comes nobody.*

Cosmology

But we are that from which draws back a thumb.
　　　　　　　　—John Berryman

When God was a little boy he stuck his finger in THE VOID.

　　THE VOID felt weird so he pulled back,
　　then in a rush to fill the space His finger left,
　　　　The Void sent out a universe in ripples.

　　God was ashamed,

　　　　so he found a world to play with,
　　　　birthed a devil out of his VOID finger,
　　formed men and women from the dust.

　　Then he abandoned his shame to us and left.

　　　　(And since,
　　　　God's history on earth is all departures.)

But it was Good!
God looked back and it was Good!
The waters tarried, the moon shone.

　　　　Even the idiot humans worked together,
　　　　　　　　　loved.

　　So God sent his Son to cover up his wrongs
　　but left him, too.

　　　　　　　　Jesus wept.

　　The God-piece of his soul departed, he was forsaken:

for the first time   a man
　　and truly alone.

　　　　(Once when I wasn't old enough to
　　　　I looked up from a creek I was following out of town
　　　　and saw God
　　　　　　　　like a tornado
　　　　sneak back from the sky into the clouds.)

And so we may draw two conclusions:

　　1) The Condition of Man is Lack of God; and

　　2) For some time God too was split, God too was made
　　　　　　　　subject to Time—

　　which is confusing because it asks us to consider
　　　　　　WHAT TIME IS
　　which if not asked, we would know

　　　　(Hours passed before I moved again.
　　　　I sat on the bank, my name erased.
　　　　No One got in close and made a promise.)

　　　　　　　　　　　Jesus spat:

　　Eloi, Eloi, lama sabachthani?

　　God doesn't know.

From the moment He first touched THE VOID,
　　He's been always on-the-go—

And so we may draw two conclusions:

God's leaving
creates the rent
through which time
issues us.

{in the beginning was the slip
of his finger}

❖ ❖ ❖

Episode I—Pilot

Every night before bed a noose is hung in the corner.
Two choices.

Shower

And then it's morning again and everything's been wiped: the going-to-bed, dinner, conversation, sex, or no-sex—all of it gone, lost. And all day I'll need to reconstitute, reconstruct, each new detail a sort of coming up for air from the shame of them, these oblivions.

In the shower they get so heavy I contort, mimic a breakdown, pull my hands and fingers through my hair as though tearing it out, lathering all the while.

(Horrible Acting)

And I know *this is important* if only for the playing out of the comedown that occurs afterwards: the admittances, the reassurances to my body—standing so the back of my neck catches the shower's spray high up, hot water splitting out across each shoulder then pooling in the crevice made by my crossed arms.

Release, Splat, Recross, Repeat.

Last night I fell asleep in my jeans, my phone still in my pocket.

I woke at two, bewildered; checked my text messages.

The last one read: hey

Honeymoon

We sit outside on the deck. We have eggs.

She knows how much salt I like to put on them.

She does it for me.

(What else could she know?)

There is an eagle and it floats in circles above us on an updraft coming off the lake's surface.

Eagles are eagle-eyed, I tell her, saying it more to myself, for myself.

She counters: Remember the one we saw driving back from Helena with the fish in its mouth—

Remember the ice cream in Helena!

Mirror-Stage

It's the sound, I don't like, the Sound of Poetry.

The pausings and the drawings out. The da-Da-da-Da-Da rhythms toiling to convince you *You* . . . are on the receiving-end of Wisdom.

Or worse: pregnant white spaces.

My [   ]

And worse than everything here I am again, writing, conjuring that sound, launching surrogate type onto surrogate paper, more as paean to an old drive than to satisfy any current ones—

(Look ma, a poem!)

All my little blue folders lined up around my Word doc; pictures of me also, on my desktop, witnessing this, embarrassed, thumbnails, little mes, little mes looking out from photos taken in Spokane or San Diego, let's-not-do-this looks pooled across their faces.

Potential author photos: ✓.

And in the photo next to these, my little nephew, Jack, half-naked and pressing himself against a mirror, recognizing, for the first time, that other—

His mouth up to his mouth, he's trying to drink himself.

"That's it, Jack," I tell him. "Get him down deep."

God if you could just be comfortable.

The Church Floor

after Herbert

Linoleum tiles: Gray, with gray ink blots
    random as any spill, any
        child's signature.

Blessed, interminable waiting
    -to-be-done-with
        The Word.

What I would not give—plagued,
    but not by ennui,
        Bored.

Not to mention all the childhood:
    time, a given;
        just to rail against.

Patience, Humility, Confidence, Charity.
  Who even understands words?
Who calls prayer ludicrous
  that is not himself,
  puffing Flesh up? Death
seeks to spoil the room,
  but cleans it:
  scrubs us with dust.

Data (II)

Plural like dust
not moose

like heat
not thunder

Not on, in, above,
or under

Of
Already

Trace and tracer
Flesh made

flesh
made flesh

Word
Eraser

Self-Portrait

I have never seen
(I have never seen
a painting)
a painting I don't like.
Even small paintings
(SMALL PAINTINGS), even
small paintings of trees I love.
Also Abstracts ~~made~~
done by the hands of teenagers.
I want one day
        (one day)
to have a portrait
painted, by a painter,
a painter of no
particular particulars
who will take my face
by its squares and
even out its bits
until the whole of it (the all
of its features)
smooths out and down to
nothing, canvas, and I am
puny, and of no
import,
fascinated
as a speck of dirt
in a small painting of teenagers.

Least

I can't tell if it's because I started to cross the street too early or because he thinks I look like whatever he thinks one looks like, or if he's just going around saying this to everyone, but when the wiry, backward-fitted-cap-wearing white dude in the SUV calls me a fucking faggot as he turns left in front of me, he means what he says, he believes it, and all the terrible feeling he has on the subject oozes toward me, seeps, like it's pooling out of his eyelids, constructing his mouth.

I at least have the good sense to flip him off as he drives past, although the glove I'm wearing robs the gesture of its more indicative features.

I walk on across after, then down the street some more where I take a left near the grocery, enter the video store, return the DVDs I'm carrying, leave, and walk a few blocks farther west to the bar where I'm to meet my work friends.

The whole way I keep looking for his car, wondering if he'll try to find me, as I was, at least, a fucking faggot who flipped him off, and there was a girl in the car.

I take my gloves off just in case and remind myself—me, who has never been in a fight save for one I lost to my little brother—that if it comes to it, I'll be ready to cross that violence-threshold, the one I've read about.

I get to the bar unscathed, explain what happened. Rochelle buys me a beer, she feels so bad for me, but what did he want, I wonder now that I've calmed a bit. I just want to ask him, what do you mean, calling me that?

Though I know I don't want him to answer, really, know I hate too; have felt that Other-feeling in the stomach, on my skin.

And know too how angry I get in the car, know I scare Kristin sometimes, the way I cuss and yell the way my mother did, does, the way her dad did too, her dad who kept a club under his seat and who once—all 5 feet 4 of him—threatened a Harlem Globetrotter for walking in front of his car then, after the Globetrotter cussed at him, shamed the man he'd just threatened into apologizing to my grandmother, who sat unnoticed in the front seat the entire time.

But Grandpa's are the good stories, the good-old stories; we think we understand him because we anecdote. We don't though, just as I don't understand the man who may *not* have gone to a bar after our confrontation, who may *not* have said: I don't know what that college faggot's problem was, he thought he could just cross the street whenever, wherever, do whatever—that everyone should just watch out for him, he's *so special*.

His Boats

By then
I will have finally washed my face in God's hands &
with my clean skin
intuit from the ligatures my fingers make
(that make my hands nervous)
there's a difference between the tulips
blooming in the garden and those
flowering in the abandoned lot.

(The same as that between
sex and death in one's
allowance to believe
one is calling all the shots.)

Much has been made of being public
in the mess of divulgence given up now to be our lot
but God's hands hold an ocean
with a private boat for each of us
where we might believe again
we are blots upon his surfaces.
Not chaff nor skim nor rot.

Ex Nihilo

for Matt Harrison

So no logistics sirens buzzing I went ballistic with the feng shui.
    Have you ever seen a room as empty-seeming?

Look at your hands: They're beautiful.
    If you would sacrifice them to the guillotine frame, we could hang
them up, call the piece, "Uselessness, the Apotheosis."

    Can we make a religion out of interior positioning?   We can.

    Can we make one out of your hands?   As long as they touch Noth-
                                         ing, but refuse temptations
                                         to make something from it.

(God tried that before, made us in the image of his wanting, left
                time's one-directional blow.)

The table looked better without the vase.
The room looked better without the table.

Remember when we moved in and the living room was just a cave
where we drank wine each night and read until one day conceitedly
I was all:

LET THERE BE A COUCH, AND A TELEVISION—

Here, let me see how your hands would look on this wall.

❖ ❖ ❖

Acknowledgments

Grateful acknowledgment to the editors of the following journals where these poems first appeared:

Faultline: "Sleeping Next to a Lion";
Juked: "Tobacco Outlet";
Connotation Press: An Online Artifact: "Breakfast Bar," "New Year's Eve Day," "Sangria."

Thank you, David St. John, for selecting this book and for being the reader I have always hoped for.

Thank you to my teachers, especially Louise Glück, Michael Ryan, and James McMichael.

Thank you to Peter Conners, Sandy Knight, Jenna Fisher, and the rest of the BOA staff for your professional guidance and your editorial and design expertise.

A very special thanks to those who helped bring this book along: Zanni Schauffler and Warren Bromley-Vogel; Patrick Coleman, Michael Barach, and Matt Harrison. Without your comments and encouragement, this book would not exist. Thank you as well to Collier Nogues, Sarah Cohen, Abby Gambrel, Ethan Rutherford, Peter Jacoby, and Kelly Wilson. You are all amazingly generous readers and thinkers and friends.

And to all my other friends scattered across the country with whom I grew up in Fort Wayne, Williamstown, DC, Irvine, Bloomington, and Moscow: Thank you. I'm tremendously lucky to know each of you.

Thank you to all my aunts, uncles, in-laws, and cousins, especially Ryan (perpetual Lake George Open runner-up) and Blake, my Magyar brother. You all have played such a large part in my life, and I am grateful that you have.

To my parents, to my brother Tyson, to Kady, Jack, Josie, and Nolan: I could not wish for a better family. Thank you for all your love and your unconditional support. I love you all very much.

And especially to Kristin: Thank you. So much.

⁓

"Plot" is dedicated to the memory of Will Neumeyer.

This book is dedicated to those included in its pages.

⁓

Citations:

Berryman, John. "Homage to Mistress Bradstreet." *Homage to Mistress Bradstreet: And Other Poems*. New York: Noonday Press, 1968.

Brainard, Joe. *I Remember*. New York: Full Court Press, 1975.

Cole, Peter. "And So the Skin . . ." *Things on Which I've Stumbled*. New York: New Directions, 2008.

Rilke, Rainer M. "Archaic Torso of Apollo." *The Selected Poetry of Rainer Maria Rilke*. Trans. Stephen Mitchell. New York: Random House, 1982.

Stevens, Wallace. "Dutch Graves in Bucks County," *Transport to Summer*. New York: Knopf, 1947.

Weil, Simone. "The *Iliad*, or the Poem of Force." *War and the Iliad*. Trans. Mary McCarthy. New York: New York Review Books, 2005.

❖ ❖ ❖

About the Author

Devin Becker was born and raised in Fort Wayne, Indiana. He currently lives in Moscow, Idaho, with his wife Kristin and their dog Rufus. He works as the digital initiatives librarian at the University of Idaho Library, maintaining and designing the library's digital collections and website. His work has been published in *American Archivist, Cutbank, Faultline, Microform and Digitization Review, Prairie Schooner,* and other journals.

❖ ❖ ❖

BOA Editions, Ltd.
The A. Poulin, Jr. New Poets of America Series

❖ ❖ ❖

Colophon

BOA Editions, Ltd., a not-for-profit publisher of poetry and other literary works, fosters readership and appreciation of contemporary literature. By identifying, cultivating, and publishing both new and established poets and selecting authors of unique literary talent, BOA brings high-quality literature to the public. Support for this effort comes from the sale of its publications, grant funding, and private donations.

The publication of this book is made possible, in part, by the special support of the following individuals:

Anonymous x 2
Armbruster Family Foundation
Angela Bonazinga & Catherine Lewis
Bernadette Catalana, *in memory of Richard Calabrese*
Gwen & Gary Conners
Jonathan Everitt
Michael Hall
Keetje Kuipers, *in memory of Maximillian Veracity Kane*
Jack & Gail Langerak
Peter & Phyllis Makuck
Daniel M. Meyers,
in honor of Steve and Phyllis Russell & Grant Holcomb
Boo Poulin, *in honor of Tyler Stofer*
Deborah Ronnen & Sherman Levey
Steven O. Russell & Phyllis Rifkin-Russell

❖ ❖ ❖